W9-BRY-751

BILL CLINTON:
President From Arkansas

BILL CLINTON:
President From Arkansas

Gene L. Martin
and
Aaron Boyd

Tudor Publishers, Inc.
Greensboro

BILL CLINTON: *President From Arkansas*

 For information write:
Tudor Publishers, Inc., P.O. Box 38366, Greensboro, North Carolina 27438 USA

Library of Congress Cataloging-in-Publication Data
Martin, Gene L.
Bill Clinton—President from Arkansas/Gene L. Martin and Aaron Boyd.—1st ed.
p. cm.
Summary: Recounts the life and political career of Bill Clinton.
ISBN 0-936389-31-1 (cloth)
1. Clinton, Bill. 1946- —Juvenile literature. 2. Presidents —
United States —Biography—Juvenile literature. [1. Clinton, Bill,
1946- . 2. Presidents] I. Boyd, Aaron 1955- . II. Title.
E886.M34 1993 .
973.929'092--dc20
[B] 93-16595
CIP
AC

Printed in the United States of America

First Edition

5 4 3 2 1

Photo credits: AP/Wide World Photos
Cover photo: AP/Wide World Photos

To Tripp, Amy, Angel, and Michael
--G.L.M.

To Sophia
--A.B.

CONTENTS

Boy From Hope

On January 20, 1993, William Jefferson Clinton was sworn in as the 42nd president of the United States of America. The ceremony, held on the West portico of the Capitol Building in Washington, D.C. was bathed in a chill but bright sunlight. A record crowd of 800,000 enthusiastic spectators witnessed the proceedings in person; the event was televised via satellite to hundreds of millions worldwide.

Although every inauguration of a U.S. President is an important event, the expectations and hopes of the United States and the world were very much focused on the tall, 46-year-old man from Arkansas who, perhaps appropriately, had been born in a small town called Hope.

The swearing-in ceremony, as well as events during the "transition period" from election day to inauguration, was symbolic of the hope and promise embodied in Bill Clinton, the first Democrat to occupy the White House since Jimmy Carter was defeated by Ronald Reagan in 1980.

After Reverend Billy Graham had performed the invocation, the choir from Philander Smith College of Little Rock, Arkansas, a mostly black institution, sang "City on the Hill." Metropolitan opera star Marilyn Horne then sang an "American Medley" celebrating diversity and "the common man."

The new president had smiled broadly throughout the ceremony, with an obvious expression of joy and confidence. Now he rose and solemnly repeated the oath of office after Supreme Court Chief Justice William Rehnquist. A new administration, and perhaps a new era in America, had begun.

In his inaugural address, President Clinton began: "This ceremony is held in the depth of Winter, but by the words we speak and the face we show the world, we force the Spring." He then challenged the country to find the "vision and courage to re-invent America." The short speech, less than 2,000 words long, held out promise for women, minorities, and the poor left out of America's bounty in the past. A second theme was a call for sacrifice from all elements of society to solve the nation's problems. "I challenge a new generation of young Americans to a season of service — to act on your idealism by helping troubled children, keeping company with those in need, reconnecting our torn communities." President Clinton went on to give his own definition of America as "an idea ennobled by the faith that our nation can summon from its myriad diversities the deepest measure of unity."

The fourteen-minute speech concluded by beckoning all citizens to join in a common effort to renew America's greatness. "We have heard the trumpets. We have changed the guard. And now—each in our own way, and with God's help—we must answer the call."

Poet Maya Angelou capped the emotion of the day with a stirring reading of her poem "On the Pulse of Morning." The poem emphasized the many ethnic, racial and religious strains which together make up the country.

Certainly, few presidents have come to power in a time of greater uncertainty about the future, and about which basic values the country should uphold. It is a time when the economic, moral, and even spiritual needs of the United States demand a strong, inspiring leader. It is an era which cries out for heroes and for heroines.

The future will show whether William Jefferson Clinton is such a leader. Who is this "man from Hope"? What are his roots? What events and trials have shaped his life and his values? What are his ideals, and how will they help shape the destiny of the United States as it enters the 21st century?

Bill Clinton never knew his father, who was killed in an automobile accident four months before Bill was born.

William Blythe III, Bill's father, was a hard-working salesman from Texas. He met a young nursing trainee named Virginia Cassidy in Shreveport, Louisiana. The romance blossomed, and soon Bill Blythe and Virginia were married. It was not long, however, before World War II intervened. The young man, like most of his friends, entered active service. Bill joined in 1942, and for most of the next three years the couple were separated as Bill served his country.

After the war, Bill Blythe returned to the sales field and went to work for a Chicago company selling earthmovers and other construction equipment. The job involved long periods of travel. When Virginia learned she was pregnant, she moved back to her hometown of Hope, Arkansas to be near her parents while her husband was on the road working.

The couple bought a house in Chicago. Bill Blythe was driving to Hope to get his wife so they could move to their new home when a tire blew out. His car swerved off the road and he drowned in a drainage ditch before help arrived.

It was a tragic blow for Virginia, who was five months pregnant. But, with the help of her parents and friends, she came through the ordeal. She was determined that her child would have a chance for a good life. When he was born, on August 19, 1946, she named the child William Jefferson Blythe IV in memory of her husband. The family soon called him Bill.

Virginia and her parents doted on the healthy, active baby and took turns caring for him. Virginia worked and the grandparents gladly pitched in to help with the raising of young Bill.

Virginia, an independent woman, wanted to further her education so that she could support her son without financial help from her parents, who were not wealthy. A hospital in New Orleans, Louisiana offered her the chance to study to become a nurse anesthetist (a specialist who puts patients to sleep before and during an operation). It was too good an opportunity to pass up, although it meant she would have to leave two-year-old Bill in the care of his grandparents while she was in school.

The separation was not easy on either mother or son. When he was three years old, his grandparents took him to visit his mother in New Orleans. Bill remembers his mother "knelt at the railroad station and wept as she put me back on the train to Arkansas with my grandmother. She endured that pain because she knew that sacrifice was the only way she could support me and give me a better life."

"My mother," Bill Clinton said as an adult, "taught me about family and hard work and sacrifice. She held steady through tragedy after tragedy. And she held our family, my brother and I, together through tough times. You want to know where I get my fighting spirit? It all started with my mother."

Although Bill missed his mother while she studied in New Orleans, he loved his maternal grandparents, especially his grandfather. He gives his grandfather much of the credit for his early training in relationships with people, and for his ability to see people as individuals, regardless of their race or income level. Years later, in his speech accepting the Democratic Presidential nomination, he said of his grandfather:

"He ran a country store in our little town of Hope.

There were no food stamps back then, so when his customers — whether they were black or white — who worked hard, did the best they could, came in with no money, well, he gave them food anyway. Just made a note of it. So did I. Before I was big enough to see over the counter, I learned from him to look up to people other folks looked down upon."

His grandparents also believed in education, although they did not have much learning themselves. They saw education as a way to improve Bill's chances of success as an adult. By the time he was three, they had taught Bill how to read and to count. Bill's grandparents were also regular church goers.

When Bill was four, Virginia finished her nurse's training and returned to Arkansas. Shortly afterward she married a car dealer named Roger Clinton. The family remained in Hope until Bill was seven, then moved to Hot Springs, Arkansas, so that Virginia could begin her nursing career.

In the 1950s the town of Hot Springs, although located deep in the "Bible Belt," retained some elements of its unusual history. A resort town near the Ouachita mountains, it had become a "wide open" town in the 1920s and 1930s, attracting an assortment of colorful—and sometimes notorious—characters, ranging from Hollywood movie stars to gangsters from the big northern cities. Tourists were drawn to Hot Springs by the gambling casinos and horse racing, as well as night clubs where big bands and famous entertainers appeared.

By the time the Clintons arrived, the city had quieted considerably, although it was still a big change from Hope. It was such a change for young Bill that Virginia thought it best that he attend a small private school when they first arrived. She was afraid Bill would have trouble adjusting to the much larger school system.

Hot Springs could have been a distracting place for a boy to grow up. But, although Virginia and Roger Clinton enjoyed an occasional evening at a night club or an afternoon at the track (Virginia is still a "two dollar" bettor), Bill was much too serious about his studies to be attracted by the night life. As a teenager, Bill went only once to the race track with his mother. He grew so bored during the afternoon, he told her that he hated the track and would never go back.

Virginia did have better luck distracting him from his studies when she took Bill to a night spot to hear the jazz trombone player Jack Teagarden. Bill sat mesmerized by the music. But, when the orchestra finished performing, he asked his mother if they could go right home.

To an outside observer, the Clinton family had no major problems. Bill's stepfather owned a local car dealership which provided a decent income. The family did not lack for material possessions. But Roger Clinton's serious drinking problem created pressures on the family. Virginia has said, "A lot of times Bill had to see behavior that was unacceptable." At times his stepfather's drinking led to violence. Once, when Bill was small, his stepfather fired a gun in the house. No one was hurt, but the bullet hole remained high on the wall for years. "I had to live with that bullet hole," Bill related in an interview. "Had to look at it every day."

Bill lived with the secret grief caused by his stepfather's problem for ten years. At times he worried about his mother's safety. When he drank, Bill would recall later, his stepfather was "consumed with self-destructive impulses." Though Bill would later come to understand his stepfather loved him deeply, and was in the grip of an addictive disease, Roger Clinton's drinking made life difficult.

Virginia was a friendly, outgoing person, interested in current events, who often voiced strong opinions about news stories. Sometimes she would sit in the kitchen and talk with Bill and some of the other kids in the neighborhood. Virginia had a strong sense of right and wrong, and often was upset when she read about a group or individual she felt was not being treated fairly.

Bill also became curious about current events. Even as a pre-teenager he read newspapers and magazines every day. As he grew older, the talks with his mother and friends became more like discussion groups. In the discussions, Virginia treated her young son as an adult, listening to his ideas and offering her own in reply. Bill became fascinated by government and how it worked.

When Bill was ten years old, his brother Roger Jr. was born. Immediately, Bill felt protective. Despite the age difference, Bill soon took Roger Jr. under his wing. Bill often babysat for his younger brother, and took him almost everywhere he went. He would even bring the toddler along on a date or outing with his friends.

Roger Sr. still had a serious problem with alcohol, and Bill wanted to spare his younger brother unpleasant scenes at home. Virginia sometimes had to work long hours and emergency shifts as a nurse at the hospital. On these occasions, Bill would stay at home to watch Roger Jr., especially if his stepfather was drinking.

"We were inseparable," Roger Jr. recalled in an interview in *The Washington Post*. "When I was little he absolutely refused to leave me anywhere." He also credits Bill with helping him come to terms with his father's alcoholism. "Bill protected me and made me aware. He helped me understand."

At fifteen, Bill changed his last name from Blythe to Clinton. People were already calling him Billy Clinton, and his mother wanted him to have the name of the man who raised him. Bill agreed, and the name change was made official.

The pressures caused by Roger Sr.'s alcoholism continued to burden the family. While drunk, Bill's stepfather became violent with Virginia. One night, when Bill was fifteen, a heated argument started in the home. Bill had seen enough. He confronted his stepfather, stepping between him and his mother. He told his stepfather that he was never to hit or abuse his mother again. By this time Bill, who was tall and heavy for his age, was physically strong enough to overpower his stepfather. Roger Clinton Sr. took the warning seriously and the beatings stopped. But, by then Virginia had had enough of the marriage; she soon filed for divorce. Bill testified at a hearing about his stepfather's violence, and the divorce was granted. However, perhaps out of compassion, Virginia later remarried Roger Clinton Sr.

Bill loved music even as a young child. He listened to popular songs on the radio, and picked out the melodies on the family piano. Always a big fan of Elvis Presley, as a teen he became a fan of Ray Charles, Dionne Warwick, and many of the artists making what became known as the "Motown" sound. Bill's musical tastes varied widely. He listened to jazz, especially saxophonists, and to folk singers, such as the group Peter, Paul and Mary.

Hot Springs High School had a great music program, and it was there that Bill began to practice with real dedication and became a first-rate saxophone player. He played in the Concert Band, the Marching Band, and the Pep Band, where he whipped up school spirit to support the teams in athletic contests. He eventually was chosen First Chair in the tenor saxophone section of the All State First Band, the highest honor he could achieve as a high school musician. There were other competitions as well, and Bill worked hard to win a first place award.

He loved the saxophone so much that even all the band activities were not enough for him. He got together with other teen musicians and played with various combo groups. One group he formed with friends was called the Three Kings. They played instrumental songs at various hometown events. In another, more sporty trio, the musicians put on dark glasses and called themselves the Three Blind Mice.

In high school, Bill was able to use his music to express his dissatisfaction over race relations in the then-segregated South. He organized an interracial group to play in a department store parking lot. In the South of that era, this was a daring venture.

Bill approached all his interests with the same intensity. He was a highly competitive student who always wanted to make the highest grade in the class. Although math was not his strongest subject, he struggled his entire junior year to outdo a classmate who was an excellent math student. When he finally accomplished his goal of scoring a higher grade, Bill came running into his house screaming about it at the top of his lungs.

Besides band activities, Bill also performed with the school theater group, was on the Student Council, belonged to the Latin Club, the Calculus Club, another math club, and the Science Club. He was also President of the Beta Club, a group for students with exceptionally high grades. Outside of school he was also involved in several groups, including the Kiwanis-sponsored Key Club. Bill did not want to excel only in the classroom and in the school band. He took part in so many activities that the school principal actually had to tell him not to join anything else. She was afraid his grades would suffer if he packed in any more extracurricular activities.

Although Bill seemed to excel in everything he tried, in at least one effort he failed miserably. A friend recalls that he and Bill had to collaborate on a special project to compete in a science fair. Bill kept telling his friend not to worry, that he had a great idea and that he would do most of the work. Just before the deadline, when it was too late to change plans, Bill brought in his "great idea" to show the partner. It turned out to be a long piece of polished steel on which Bill had placed a hot dog. The device was called a "solar powered" hot dog cooker. The sun was supposed to heat the metal and cook the hot dog. Needless to say, the device did not work, and the pair did not win the prize.

Bill's extracurricular activities provided him with his first real taste of politics. In 1963, at the age of sixteen, the local branch of the American Legion invited him to be part of Boys' State, a program for young leaders. Bill, along with a few others, attended the national convention, called Boys' Nation, in Washington, D.C., the nation's capital. There, two things happened that would have a tremendous impact on Bill's future. He met and had lunch with Arkansas Senator J. William Fulbright, one of the nation's most respected and powerful leaders. Senator Fulbright inspired him and would later help Bill begin his career.

However, the most exciting and impressive moment of the trip came when the boys were taken to the White House Rose Garden to meet President John F. Kennedy, Bill's idol. It was a critical point in his life. He had been uncertain about what career to pursue as an adult. Now he knew. His mother saw that his mind was made up as soon as he returned home: "When he came back from Washington, holding this picture of himself with Jack Kennedy, and the expression on his face, I knew right then he would make his career in government." Although he had already been active in school politics, and had served as junior class president, the visit with Kennedy, only weeks before he was assassinated in Dallas, sealed Bill's future. He would be a politician.

But the young man still found time to be a typical teenager. In addition to his music groups and other activities, Bill enjoyed sports. He had a tendency to put on weight, and was also a little clumsy and a slow runner. He clearly never was going to be a star at athletics. But he approached sports with his typical energy. Bill put up a basketball hoop at his house and played pickup games by the hour with his friends. He especially loved football, but was hampered by his slowness. He also liked to bowl and play miniature golf. His non-athletic hobbies included crossword puzzles, watching old movies on t.v., and reading. Mystery novels were a favorite.

Bill graduated from high school in 1964 with high honors. He credits excellent teachers for his academic success in high school. "They made us work hard, and they gave hard tests," he remembers, and credits high expectations with helping him to excel. He believes he got a first-rate education in the Hot Springs public school system, especially in English and mathematics. Even many years later, he could quote long passages from *Macbeth*, as he proved by reciting from the play by heart during a talk at a Vilonia, Arkansas high school in 1990.

As graduation day for the Class of 1964 approached, Bill had to choose a college. Although he considered attending the University of Arkansas, he wanted a school with a good program in foreign relations. He asked a school guidance counselor which college offered the best education in that field. Without hesitation, she recommended Georgetown University, located in Washington D.C. Bill was delighted. He had "fallen in love" with Washington during his Boys' Nation visit. Although Georgetown was an expensive private school, and he would have to work part-time in order to meet the expenses, he left for Washington D.C. in the fall of 1964 confident that he had made the right decision.

Traveling Scholar

Bill had barely unpacked his bags at Georgetown before he began running for president of the freshman class. Using a style that was to become second nature to him, he met as many people as possible, shaking hands and talking about his ideas concerning school government. Even students who did not care about school politics often were impressed with his intelligence and determination. Two competitors for the office ended their own campaigns and voted for Bill! He won the election.

One issue which concerned Bill was the high price of food in the student cafeteria. He had little money himself, and in fact needed a job to help pay his tuition. The only person he knew in Washington was Senator Fulbright, whom Bill had met two years before while attending Boys' Nation. Bill was given a job as an administrative and research assistant in Senator Fulbright's office. It was part-time work, but paid $8,500 over the next year, more than enough to help his mother put him through his first year of college.

With studies, student politics, and his job working on Capitol Hill, Bill's first year at Georgetown passed quickly. Even with his many outside interests, Bill made the spring Dean's List and earned an A- average.

The next year Bill was elected sophomore class president. He quickly gained a reputation for assisting students. One of these was freshman Harold Snider, a blind student whom Bill helped learn his way around campus.

The four years Bill spent at Georgetown were turbulent ones for the United States. The Civil Rights movement created tensions in cities all over the country, especially in Bill's native South. Also, beginning in the summer of 1964, President Lyndon Johnson began sending more and more men and women to fight in Vietnam. Americans had divided feelings concerning each of these developments. The events that occurred during Bill's years in Georgetown forced everyone, especially college students, to decide what they believed about issues students in years past did not have to worry about.

The Civil Rights movement was the struggle of African-Americans to gain the same rights as other Americans, such as the right to vote, or to have an equal education. The laws denying equal rights were popular among some white citizens, and the efforts of African-Americans to gain full citizenship were long and bitter. Bill had strong beliefs about civil rights. He thought the way African-Americans had been treated over the years, especially in his native South, needed to be changed. As a teenager, Bill had memorized long passages from civil rights leader Martin Luther King Jr.'s famous "I Have A Dream" speech. When Dr. King was assassinated in April of 1968, riots erupted in many large cities, including Washington. Bill signed up to work with a local group to bring food and medical supplies to people caught in the riot.

The war in Vietnam was an equally divisive issue for all Americans. The United States became involved in the conflict when the communist government of North Vietnam attempted to overthrow the pro-American government of South Vietnam. While American leaders believed it was in the national interest to stop the spread of communism, other Americans thought the United States should not become involved in a war thousands of miles away. Having grown up in a conservative part of the country, Bill supported the war in the beginning. But as the fighting dragged on, he began to change his beliefs. One of his jobs in Senator Fulbright's office was to search through the weekly lists of dead soldiers for the names of Arkansas natives, so Senator Fulbright could send a personal letter of condolence to the family. Bill quickly became aware of the cost of the war.

Vietnam was a constant subject of discussion among the students at Georgetown. As Bill became more convinced the war was wrong, he started expressing his opinions to others. The war also had a personal impact. The U.S. government had put into place a draft, or mandatory military service. As the war in Vietnam escalated, the army needed more and more young men to fight. The draft hung over the heads of males of Bill's generation. While attending Georgetown, Bill had a student deferment which protected him from the draft. But, unless he attended graduate school, he would no longer have a deferment.

A family matter brought Bill sadness during his final period at Georgetown. His stepfather was dying of cancer. Bill found time every weekend to drive the three hundred miles south to Durham, North Carolina to visit Roger Clinton Sr. as he underwent treatment at Duke University Medical Center. The elder Clinton had finally stopped drinking toward the end of his life, and he and Bill had made peace.

"There was nothing else to fight over," Bill said years later about his visits with his stepfather, "nothing else to run from. It was a wonderful time in my life, and I think in his." After his stepfather died later in the year, Bill volunteered to work as a student counselor in a clinic for people struggling with alcoholism. Bill realized the addiction had been the great tragedy of his stepfather's life.

In the midst of all this personal and public activity, Bill finished his undergraduate education at Georgetown. Although he lost a race for President of Student Council in 1967, he remained popular with fellow students and teachers. His grades continued to be high. When a classmate suggested to him that he apply for a Rhodes Scholarship to Oxford University in England, Bill at first did not think he could win. But Senator Fulbright agreed to recommend him, and he decided to apply for the scholarship. The Clintons were overjoyed when Bill received word he had been selected as a Rhodes Scholar. He was only the second student in Georgetown's history to receive the honor. Things were looking up for the boy from Arkansas.

However, there was a problem. As Bill left for Oxford, President Johnson repealed the draft deferment for graduate students. Bill's Oxford education could be cut short if he received a draft notice. He would have to give up his scholarship, return to the United States, and perhaps help fight a war he did not believe in.

Rhodes Scholars traditionally sailed to England. On the ship Bill quickly began making friends. He heard about a fellow scholar who was seasick in his cabin. Bill took chicken soup and visited with him. The young student, Robert Reich, became a lifelong friend. Years later, when President Bill Clinton selected his cabinet, he named Robert Reich to serve as Secretary of Labor. Other friends Bill made at Oxford included Robert Rubin, one of his top economic advisors, and Strobe Talbott, an ambassador to the former Soviet Union.

Bill's years at Oxford were different from his years at Georgetown. Because there were no student politics or part-time jobs to take up his time, Bill threw himself into the political and philosophical arguments Oxford encouraged.

Bill and his friends did bring one topic of discussion with them from America. The war and the draft were still a part of everyone's life. When Bill arrived at Oxford in the fall of 1968, he found an induction notice from his draft board waiting for him. However, because of the time spent on the slow sea voyage, his induction date had passed. When he called the draft board, they decided to allow him to remain in Oxford for the rest of the year.

Despite the tensions over the draft and the war, Bill made the most out of his Oxford experience. Tall and easygoing, he contrasted strongly with the tradition-steeped students and faculty of Oxford's University College. But, as usual, his friendliness won over almost everyone he met. Even Douglas the Porter, a former Sergeant Major in the British Army, whose job it was to see that the grounds were maintained and to preside over the dormitory, was charmed. Douglas was notoriously upright, a man with a "stiff upper lip," who had little use for students, except to see that they behaved in the approved Oxford manner. Amazed fellow students still remember Douglas and Bill sitting around the Porter's Lodge, exchanging stories and acting as though they had known one another for years.

Bill and his friends would often stay up late at night drinking coffee and discussing a wide variety of topics while listening to music. He often hitchhiked into London to see a play or to visit the art museums.

Sometimes, he would walk through the countryside around Oxford, taking in the lovely scenery. He and his friends varied their on-campus meals in the dining hall with forays to Chinese or Indian restaurants. Bill was very fond of what he considered the English equivalent of a big southern breakfast—fried eggs, tomato slices, bacon and mushrooms—which he enjoyed at a cafe in the Covered Market area of Oxford.

Bill even tried out for the Oxford basketball team, along with a number of other Americans. Few of them could rebound or play good defense, and Bill remained notoriously slow. But basketball is a minor sport in Great Britain, about as popular as cricket in the United States. Even with his limitations, Bill had a chance to make the starting team, until he decided his studies and other activities did not leave him enough time for basketball. The Oxford basketball team had been started years earlier by Rhodes Scholar Bill Bradley. Bradley had been an All-American at Princeton, who went on to be an NBA star before retiring and winning election to the U.S. Senate from New Jersey.

Bill thrived in the free-spirited intellectual atmosphere of the college. Discussions ranged over a wide variety of topics, including politics, religion, public policy, history and music. Oxford allowed Bill an opportunity, for once, to slow down his pace and spend time doing things simply because he enjoyed them.

Back in Arkansas for the summer of 1969, Bill was again faced with the draft. To receive a deferment, he enrolled in the University of Arkansas Law School and joined the Reserve Officers Training Corps, or ROTC. This way he hoped to finish law school and, hopefully, the war would be over before he graduated.

But in the fall, Bill changed his mind and decided to return to Oxford to continue his Rhodes Scholarship. During Bill's second year at Oxford, President Richard Nixon began a lottery system. In this system, the higher the number the young man received in the annual lottery, which was based on his birthday, the lesser his chances were of being drafted. Bill received a high lottery number, and was not drafted.

The events surrounding his draft status would cause Bill trouble in the years to come. Friends who knew Bill at Oxford remember that he anguished over the draft, and was undecided about what to do. He wanted to continue his education. Also, he was opposed to the war in Vietnam, and felt a moral obligation not to fight in a war he and millions of other Americans believed wrong.

Bill finally decided that putting his name back in the draft and taking his chances on being drafted was the honorable thing to do. Many other young men took more drastic steps to avoid the draft. An Oxford friend, with whom Bill had many conversations about the war, later resisted the draft and remained in England.

The war cast a shadow over Bill's Oxford years. As he later explained it: "My antiwar feelings were particularly painful to me at first, because I never was anti-military in the sense that a lot of people were. One of the most precious memories of my childhood is my mother trying to get me to know my dead father, showing me a presidential citation he'd received for good duty in the war. I was proud of that. I wanted to be part of my country's defense and my country's service."

Toward the end of his second year at Oxford, Bill began thinking it was time to leave. Although the scholarship was for three years, and Bill had not finished his graduate degree in Politics, he decided to return to the United States and attend Yale Law School in New Haven, Connecticut. His decision was made easier when Yale offered him a scholarship.

Bill started Yale Law School in the fall of 1970. As usual, it took him only a few days to begin making friends. He was certainly no regular Southerner at Yale. There were only a few African-American students at Yale Law School. Feeling outnumbered, and perhaps out of place, most of the African-American students ate together at one table in the cafeteria. White students assumed they were not welcome at the table, and stayed away. It was a sort of segregation by choice, and all the students followed the unwritten rule. All the students except Bill Clinton. William Coleman III, a black student from Detroit who later became one of Bill's roommates, recalls a young man with a "thick southern accent and a cherubic face who would unceremoniously violate the unspoken taboo by plopping himself at the black table." Although it took a while for the African-American students to get used to him, Bill became something of a regular at the table, telling stories and cracking jokes with his friendly drawl until he had won over the minority students. "In matters of race and racism the heart will usually prevail over the head and, in this regard, there simply is no question about Bill's heart," Coleman says.

Bill's talent for telling stories about life in Arkansas kept his friends laughing. The first time Hillary Rodham became aware of the man who would later become her husband, she heard a loud, booming voice in a student lounge at Yale saying: "And not only that, we have the largest watermelons in the world!" It turned out to be Bill Clinton, educating some other students about his favorite topic, Arkansas. Although it was not the most romantic setting, Hillary took notice of the tall Southerner and thought she would like to get to know him.

Luckily, the two had one class together. Bill had noticed Hillary too, and sometimes would follow her at a distance after class was over, but did not have the courage to start a conversation. But one evening both were trying to study in the law library. Bill kept glancing up from his work, sneaking looks at the young woman he was enchanted with from a distance. Hillary knew he was staring at her. Finally, she decided to take matters in her own hands and left her books to walk over to Bill. "Look," she said, "if you're going to keep staring at me and I'm going to keep staring back, I think we should at least know each other's names. I'm Hillary Rodham. What's your name?"

Bill was so surprised by Hillary's approach that he could not remember his name. "I was so embarrassed," he said later. "I was real impressed that she did that."

After their abrupt introduction in the library, Hillary met Bill again as she was registering for the next semester's classes. "He joined me in this long line, and we talked for an hour." When they got to the registration table, a sheepish Bill was reminded that he had already registered.

Hillary Rodham, a year younger than Bill, was born in 1947 in Chicago, Illinois. She had grown up and attended school in Park Ridge, a wealthy suburb of Chicago.

The Rodhams were determined that their children would grow up with both the work ethic and a sense of public service. As children, they had individual chores, such as picking dandelions out of the yard at a penny each. Parents Hugh and Dorothy made a special trip to West Virginia to show the children the coal-mining area where Hugh had worked so hard as a young man during the Depression of the 1930s.

Brothers Hugh and Tony were hard put to keep up with the studious Hillary. "At school, people sure expected a lot from Hillary's brothers," recalls Hugh. Tony went on to attend Iowa Wesleyan College, while Hugh played football at Penn State, graduating in 1972. After graduation, he joined the Peace Corps for two years in Columbia.

Hillary earned every possible Girl Scout badge. As a teenager, she worked at a city park, lugging sports equipment back and forth each day. She served as president of her senior class, and received so many awards at her graduation that her parents recall being somewhat embarrassed as she was repeatedly called to the podium. She also found time to organize circuses and amateur sports tournaments to raise money for migrant workers. "Mothers in the neighborhood were amazed at how they couldn't get their boys to do much," recalls a friend, "but Hillary had them all running around."

Hillary attended Wellesley, a prestigious woman's college located in Massachusetts. She was elected student body president during her senior year, and graduated with honors in 1969.

Hillary was the first student in the history of Wellesley to address her class during graduation ceremonies. In her address, she expressed a commitment to public service, one which she still maintains. In the years before college, Hillary had changed her political beliefs. Her family had always been conservative, preferring to vote for Republican candidates in elections. Hillary herself had been a so-called "Goldwater Girl," an avid supporter of conservative Republican nominee Barry Goldwater in the 1964 U.S. presidential campaign. But as she grew older she became more liberal in her beliefs, especially when she saw for herself the extremes of poverty in some Chicago neighborhoods.

Bill shared a cottage on Fort Trumball Beach with other law students. Shortly after they met in the library, Hillary was visiting the cottage for games of volleyball and touch football on the beach. Hillary quickly became close to Bill's friends. In a short time, she joined the late night discussions the group enjoyed.

In 1972, the Democratic Party nominated Senator George McGovern for president. Bill and Hillary spent the summer and fall working for him. Bill was a director of the McGovern campaign in Texas. Although McGovern was easily defeated by Richard Nixon, Bill made a great impression on his fellow campaign workers.

Bill's last year at Yale was 1973, another decisive year for America. Secretary of State Henry Kissinger finally concluded a peace agreement which brought an end to American fighting in Vietnam. At the same time, President Nixon watched his administration fall apart because of the Watergate scandal. "Watergate" involved a series of crimes which some of President Nixon's 1972 campaign staff committed in their efforts to make his reelection certain. Also in 1973, the Supreme Court handed down the *Roe vs. Wade* decision, which instructed the states they could no

In 1972, Bill worked in George McGovern's campaign for president. He is seen here with McGovern and Arkansas Democratic Party Chief Joe Purcell (right) at Little Rock airport.

As the youngest governor in the country, 34 year old Bill Clinton sought re-election in 1980.

longer pass laws to make abortion illegal. These events of 1973 were all highly controversial.

Bill faced more personal decisions. With his brilliant school record, he easily could have moved to New York or Washington and become a wealthy lawyer, high-level congressional staff person, or a clerk on the Supreme Court. These were the career paths chosen by most of his fellow law school students, and was the type of career Hillary planned. But Bill's needs were different: "I promised myself a long time ago, that if the people of Arkansas would let me, that I would break my back to help my state. That's my life, and that's the way it has to be for me."

In the spring of 1973, Bill and Hillary graduated from Yale Law School. It was a time for painful decisions. Both wondered if Hillary would be happy living in the small, mostly rural state of Arkansas. Hillary even had her doubts if Bill himself could truly be happy back home. He had lived outside of Arkansas for almost nine years. Virginia Clinton knew her son was going through a difficult decision about leaving Hillary. "He loved Hillary so much," she recalls. Hillary decided to go to Cambridge, Massachusetts, to work for the Children's Defense Fund. Later, she moved to Washington, where she got a job on the congressional staff investigating the possible impeachment of President Nixon for his part in the Watergate scandal.

Bill, determined to follow through on the decision he had made years before, headed home. He was 27 years old.

Young Governor Clinton

Although his long-term goal was to enter politics, Bill had to earn a living. One of his Yale professors had suggested that he apply for a job on the teaching staff at the University of Arkansas Law School in Fayetteville. At first Bill did not think he wanted to teach. He planned to open a small law practice in Hot Springs.

But opening a law office, even a small one, takes money. On the drive south from New Haven, Bill changed his mind. He stopped at a telephone booth and called the dean of the law school to ask for a job. Bill agreed to teach any course that needed an instructor. Impressed, the dean gave him a job.

Bill was an enthusiastic teacher. He enjoyed the job and easily could have made a career as a law professor. But Bill had decided on a career in public service years before. And he had always exhibited a determination to stick with his goals.

But, how was he to start his career? If he were defeated overwhelmingly in his first run for office, he might never have another chance. He also wanted to attain an office that would allow him to improve the lives of the people of Arkansas.

Arkansas is a poor state, with one of the lowest average incomes in the country. It also has a long history of racial oppression toward African-Americans. In 1957, President Eisenhower had to call out Federal troops to force then-Governor Orval Faubus to allow nine black students to attend Central High School in Little Rock. The confrontation between Faubus and Eisenhower was a national scandal. Television images of white thugs pushing and hitting the black citizens of Little Rock created an image in the minds of most Americans which Bill and other progressive Arkansans wanted to change.

Bill decided that a run for the U.S. House of Representatives in the Third Congressional District would be the best way to begin his political career. But running against the Republican incumbent, John Paul Hammerschmidt, was not going to be easy. Hammerschmidt was always careful to respond to any letter or complaint received from one of his constituents, and was widely popular. Furthermore, most people in Arkansas are conservative. Bill knew that they would not easily replace a well-liked representative.

Nevertheless, Bill announced his decision to be the Democratic candidate for the seat, and threw himself into the race. Immediately, people were impressed by his limitless energy, his enthusiasm, and his evident love of campaigning. Bill would dive into a crowd of voters and make sure anyone who wanted to shake his hand had the opportunity. One visitor to the campaign remembers riding to the airport with Bill. The candidate sighted ten men working on the street and had the driver stop the car. "There are ten votes," he said, bounding out of the car.

Bill's chances were improved when Republican President Nixon resigned in August of 1974 because of the Watergate affair. All Republicans had a difficult time that year as Americans responded angrily to Watergate. Gradually, the confident Hammerschmidt began to get nervous. But, even with the Watergate scandal helping him, Bill had an uphill fight. Hammerschmidt had the support of the political and business establishment. Most observers expected Bill to be soundly defeated.

More and more people were impressed enough to

come over to Bill's campaign. His reputation as a hard-working, intelligent young man spread. Bill gave speeches on a wide range of issues. He spoke out for better schools, and received the endorsement of the Arkansas Education Association. He promised that, if elected, he would make the U.S. House of Representatives "stand up and do what it is supposed to do." Bill also attempted to express in words the way most Americans felt toward the Federal government: "The American people have a general feeling of helplessness about the federal bureaucracy, which is unyielding, distant, and not responsible."

Bill also sounded a theme which he would continue right through the 1992 campaign. "People want a hand up," he said repeatedly, "not a handout."

Hundreds of people were attracted to his campaign. One new campaign worker, however, was an old ally. When President Nixon resigned, Hillary's staff position in Washington came to an end. She decided to move to Arkansas and teach at the law school so she could be near Bill. Her friends remember being shocked when she told them of her decision. When asked why she would leave a successful career in Washington, Hillary gave a simple answer: "I love him."

In Arkansas, Hillary quickly discovered she appreciated a small-town atmosphere. "I liked people tapping me on the shoulder at the grocery store and saying, 'Aren't you that lady professor at the law school?'"

Hillary quickly realized Bill's congressional campaign needed her help. While Bill had definite political ideas, his campaign style was chaotic. He would return to his Fayetteville bungalow from campaigning with pockets filled with scraps of paper on which he had hastily jotted down names of supporters he had met. Hillary took one look at the jumble of paper on his desk and immediately set to work organizing his headquarters, schedule and speeches. Bill quickly acknowledged Hillary's political talents, telling reporters that she was "far better organized, more in control, more intelligent and more eloquent than I am."

Bill also met the Rodham family. Although it took some time before the Rodhams adjusted to his southern accent, a close bond quickly formed between them. "If he was good enough for Hillary, he was certainly good enough for us," said brother Tony.

The Rodhams liked Bill so well they moved to Fayetteville and took an apartment, which became Bill's unofficial campaign headquarters. Hugh Sr. answered the telephone, while Hugh Jr. and Tony drove through the district nailing up posters.

Despite all the hard work, Bill would not be going to Congress in 1974. Hammerschmidt, who had easily been winning reelection since 1966, squeaked through with 51.8% of the vote.

Bill still calls the unsuccessful 1974 House race "the best campaign I ever ran, a just cause that I almost won. I discovered what I like about politics. You learn something. You hear another life story at every stop."

After the campaign, Hugh and Dorothy returned to Oak Park. But Hugh Jr. followed Hillary's advice and stayed in Fayetteville to continue his studies at the university, receiving two advanced degrees in education and a law degree.

Bill learned much about Arkansas politics during the 1974 race. He made many friends and allies in the 24 counties making up the Third District. He also learned that he was a born politician. There would be no looking back for Bill Clinton.

But there were other personal considerations to be taken care of before his next political campaign. After Hillary joined him in Fayetteville, they grew even closer. Friends remember them as an impressive young couple. Hillary fit easily into the law school faculty, taught Criminal Law and other courses, and was praised for her teaching skills.

On a hot August day in 1975, Hillary returned to Fayetteville after visiting her parents in Chicago. Bill picked her up at the airport. She noticed that he was not taking the usual route back to her apartment. When Hillary asked where they were going, Bill gave her a strange answer: "I bought that house you like," he said.

Hillary was mystified, and asked him what house he was talking about. Bill reminded her that a few days before her trip to Chicago she had noticed a small house for sale and remarked that it was pretty. Hillary remembered the house, but reminded him that she had never been inside it.

Bill said. "Well, I bought it. So I guess we'll have to get married now."

Hillary accepted his untraditional proposal, and did love the house. The small bungalow had lovely vaulted ceilings and a bay window. However, Bill and his friends had to rush to paint it before the wedding.

Bill and Hillary were married on October 11, 1975. They both wanted a small, private ceremony, so the wedding was held in the freshly painted house. Bill's brother Roger was his best man. Hillary, for the time being, kept her maiden name of Rodham.

The next day the couple held a reception for

friends and political supporters. Over two hundred people showed up. One guest was Arkansas Attorney General, Jim Guy Tucker. The Attorney General represents the state in court and works closely with law enforcement. Tucker, who was not going to run for reelection, spent most of the reception trying to convince Bill that he should run for Attorney General. Even Bill and Hillary's wedding reception was a political event.

After the wedding and the reception, Bill and Hillary left for their honeymoon. With their mutual enjoyment of unorthodox behavior, there was no way the Clintons were going to have a normal honeymoon. First, they picked up Hugh Jr. and Tony, then Hillary's parents, before going to Acupulco for ten days.

Although the close race for Congress had helped Bill's statewide reputation, he knew he needed to win his next race. Another loss might ruin his career. Bill decided to run for Attorney General, and was determined to win. He announced his intentions on April 1, 1976.

Initially, police officers in the state had doubts about the young law professor who wanted to be the state's top cop. They feared he would not be tough enough on crime issues. But Bill assured them he supported the death penalty for criminals who kill police officers. They became enthusiastic supporters.

The Attorney General's race turned out to be much easier than the House campaign. Bill easily won the Democratic primary, gaining 60% of the vote. No Republican even attempted to stop him. He ran unopposed in the fall campaign. In January of 1977, Bill was sworn in to his first political office. He was thirty years old.

Bill saw his mission as Attorney General to be one of working to pass stronger ethics laws for politicians to follow, and to fight the utility companies he felt were raising prices unfairly. Although he was Attorney General for only two years, he worked eighty hour weeks pushing his ideas. Bill made sure the people of Arkansas knew about his efforts on their behalf by issuing regular reports. Arkansans reacted positively to his efforts, and Bill's popularity grew.

Bill's ambition was to seek still higher office. When Senator John McClellan died and left an open U. S. Senate seat, many of Bill's supporters wanted him to run for that job. Although the Senate seat would be more prestigious, Bill knew he had returned to Arkansas to work for the people of his state. He could do that best by running for Governor in 1978.

With his high popularity and the campaign organization he had established in the two earlier races, Bill easily won the Democratic primary. In the general election, he came under attack by some newspaper columnists and political opponents for being too liberal. His enemies said that his years in Ivy League schools, his opposition to the Vietnam War, his support for the Equal Rights Amendment (a proposed amendment to the U.S. Constitution which would make discrimination against women illegal) and the fact Hillary had kept her maiden name, proved that Bill did not fit into conservative Arkansas. But Bill answered the attacks in a good-natured manner, and continued talking about education reform and bringing down the high rates people had to pay for electricity.

Bill won the election, earning 63.4% of the vote. At age 32, he became the youngest governor in the United States, and the second youngest governor in history.

It had been almost easy up to this point. But that would change very soon.

The move from the couple's bungalow to the Governor's Mansion was emotionally difficult. Despite the excitement of winning the election, it was a sad time for Bill and Hillary, signaling a close to a very happy period in their life together. "We had a wonderful life there," Hillary remembers fondly.

"Long conversations with friends and dinners that went on for hours where you talked about everything that was going on in your life and in the world."

Bill's election as governor brought him national recognition. Young and handsome, he made a great news story. There was already talk he might be a vice-presidential candidate in 1980, although Bill would not be old enough to legally qualify for the job until 1981.

It was surprising for the first term governor of a small state to receive so much attention. Arkansas is about the size of New York state in land mass, but is only one-fourth the size of New York City in population. Bill himself said that his run for the governor's office was "a little bit like running for class president." For Bill to receive so much national attention was clear evidence of his potential as a future leader.

Bill was anxious to hit the ground running in his new job. In his inaugural address, he said: "We have an opportunity to forge a future that is more remarkable, rich and fulfilling to all Arkansans than our proud past. We must not squander it."

Bill hired a young, brilliant and hardworking staff. However, many of them were not native to the state. They tried to force Arkansas into meeting their idea of a progressive state, ignoring the feelings of the

A young governor Clinton observes a 1983 training exercise of the Arkansas National Guard at Fort Chaffee.

people they were trying to lead.

In education, for example, Bill and his aides pushed the legislature to increase funds. Arkansas teachers were the lowest-paid in the country. Bill wanted higher teacher salaries. Another education problem was the unequal distribution of money among school districts. The young governor proposed merging school systems to help equalize the way education money was spent.

Bill pushed through a statewide test all new teachers had to pass before beginning their careers. Also, tests were required for all Arkansas students, to determine how well the school system was performing. Other reforms included the establishment of a Governor's School for gifted students, and increased funding for vocational education.

Clearly, Bill had a large agenda, and education was only one area. To improve the badly deteriorated highway system, Bill had to find a way to raise money. One method was to raise state fees for auto license tags. This was very unpopular in a poor rural state.

Other changes Bill attempted dealt with reforming the way utility rates were raised, and installing rural health clinics. In every reform Bill tried to put in place, he was attacked by powerful interest groups.

They tried to convince conservative Arkansas citizens that Bill was not really one of them. Over and over, in newspaper editorials and other media, Hillary was portrayed as a Northern feminist who had not taken her husband's name. Bill was also accused of seeking to legalize drugs and control the ownership of guns. Early in his administration, Bill realized he had many powerful enemies.

Things would get worse. Democratic President Jimmy Carter was becoming increasingly unpopular. Inflation was high, and a revolution in Iran decreased oil imports, creating long lines at gas pumps. This caused driving to be more expensive, and made the increased license fees seem even worse. Then, Cuban dictator Fidel Castro indirectly created Bill's biggest political headache.

When 120,000 Cubans were allowed to leave Cuba for the U.S. in 1980, President Carter welcomed them. Many of the Cubans were fleeing oppression. But Castro also emptied his prisons and allowed criminals to join the others seeking freedom.

Bill and President Carter were friends. When Carter decided to house some of the Cubans at Fort Chaffee, Arkansas, Bill did not resist. He could not stop the housing of the Cubans, and he felt all Americans should do their part to help deal with the problem.

Many Arkansans did not want the Cubans in their state. People were outraged when several hundred detainees escaped Fort Chaffee in May, 1980. Then, in June, Fort Chaffee erupted into a riot. Fear spread throughout Arkansas. Although Bill called out the National Guard and the rioters were stopped, he was blamed for the violence. His popularity fell.

Bill's staff continued to be a problem. They were devoted to doing a good job, but they were not very diplomatic in dealing with the legislature. Many state politicians felt they were "hippies," and some even called them the "bearded ones," because several wore beards. These aides also made themselves unpopular by lecturing the people of Arkansas and their representatives. Many citizens were offended by their manner.

All these problems, along with the declining popularity of Democrats nationally, hurt Bill politically. If Arkansas had elections every four years, as did most states, his chances of reelection would have been better. However, in Arkansas the governor served a two year term, and Bill would have to run for reelection in 1980. (Arkansas changed its state constitution in the 1980s; now, governors serve four-year terms.) Bill's political troubles mounted, and his popularity declined. 1980 was not shaping up to be a good year.

One happy event did take place that year. On February 27, Hillary gave birth to a daughter. Bill and Hillary had attended natural childbirth classes, but they did not get to use the method. The baby was positioned wrongly in the womb and had to be delivered by caesarian section. The little girl, however, was healthy. Bill walked the hospital corridors all night, holding the new baby. Bill and Hillary named their daughter Chelsea, after one of their favorite Judy Collins songs, "Chelsea Morning."

Chelsea's birth had a profound impact on Bill. It brought back memories of his own childhood, and the father he never knew. "I remember when my daughter was born," he said later, "maybe the greatest night of my life. I remember thinking a few minutes after she was born, this is something my father never got to feel." Although both Bill and Hillary said they wanted more children, Chelsea is their only child.

Bill's joy at being a new father was interrupted by the reelection campaign. Despite easily defeating a challenger for the Democratic nomination, the general election was more difficult. His opponent, Frank White, changed his party affiliation to run against Bill. The slogan White used against Bill was "Cubans and Car Tags." He attacked Clinton for being too liberal and too young. Nationally, 1980 was a Republican year, and Ronald Reagan was extremely popular in Arkansas. Bill fought back, calling White a tool of those who wanted to stop progress in the state.

But it was no use. White won the election by 35,000 votes, out 840,000 cast. Bill had gone from being the youngest governor in the country, to the youngest ex-governor, in two short years.

Bill was shocked. The morning after the election he appeared with Hillary and Chelsea on the steps of the state capitol. He admitted he had shed tears over the defeat. "But we accept the will of our people with humility and with gratitude for having been given a chance to serve our state."

Virginia said afterward she was more proud of Bill at this moment of defeat than at any other time in his life. "The way Bill accepted defeat was the proudest I've ever been of him."

Despite his courage and good grace in losing, friends recall that Bill became depressed. For the first time in his life, he seemed to have no specific goal or plan of action for the future. He and Hillary took an extended trip to the Holy Land, where Bill found solace visiting sites described in the Bible. The trip was good for his spirits. He returned to Little Rock in a more upbeat mood, and soon talked of winning his old job back. He joined the Little Rock law firm of Wright, Lindsey and Jennings, and began working with his usual energy on cases involving commerce and business.

After leaving the governor's mansion in 1980, Hillary worked for a Little Rock law firm, and was twice named among the top 100 lawyers in the country by the *National Law Journal*. She found time to serve on seventeen civic and corporate boards.

Bill's reputation was partially restored by his participation in an annual event called "The Farkleberry Follies." The purpose of the event was to poke fun at, or "roast," prominent individuals. The theme of the show was "Cubans and Car Tags," and Bill was the surprise guest. He gave a humorous speech about himself and Frank White, who was in the audience and joined in the fun. Arkansans admired Bill's ability to joke about himself so shortly after a political setback.

Many people started reaping the benefits of the changes Bill had pushed through as governor. The car tag fee increase helped improve highways. Education improved as more money flowed into state classrooms. People realized that Bill had been the primary cause of these improvements.

Bill traveled around the state. He gave speech after speech criticizing Governor White for allowing utility rate increases, and for taking credit for the improvements Bill had worked to attain. Soon after White became governor, a bumper sticker that read "Don't blame me—I voted for Clinton" began popping up on automobiles all over Arkansas.

The speeches did something else as well. Bill never missed a chance to apologize for the mistakes in his first term. As the 1982 governor's race began, Bill's new slogan was: "You can't lead without listening." It was his way of letting the people of Arkansas know he had learned from his mistakes.

Bill campaigned hard. At stop after stop, he said: "I was too inflexible in my first term. This is a very personal state that requires me to be accessible to the people. I promise to correct my past mistakes." Bill realized he must create consensus for his programs.

White attacked Bill as he had in 1980. His campaign commercials called Bill "soft" on crime, and hinted Bill was not a true Arkansan. Not to be outdone, Bill characterized White as a pawn of the wealthy.

Hillary did what she could to help Bill's chances for election. She had been criticized for keeping her maiden name, and decided now to legally change it to Clinton. When a reporter asked what her new name was going to be, Hillary quipped: "I think Martha Washington sounds nice." The line got a great laugh, and won over women tired of the name issue.

On election day, Bill earned 54.7% of the vote. He was the first Arkansas governor to regain office after being voted out. In his January inaugural address, Bill thanked the voters for giving him a second chance. He promised to govern with a "profound sense of humility."

National Spotlight

In the space of two short years, Bill had tasted both defeat and victory. He decided to avoid the mistakes which had cost him the 1980 election. One mistake was trying to accomplish too much, too fast. He carefully listed the most important priorities. At the top of the list was education reform. He decided to focus on that issue.

Education was on many minds in 1983. The National Commission on Excellence in Education had issued a report on the nation's schools ominously entitled "A Nation At Risk." The report spoke of a "rising tide of mediocrity" and cited education reform as the foremost problem facing Americans. In Arkansas, the state Supreme Court had ordered a more equitable distribution of funds among state schools.

Bill realized he needed to create agreement among the people before he sought legislation to reform the schools. He formed a committee to meet with parents, teachers, and other experts, and to report their findings. Bill picked as chairperson of the committee someone he knew he could trust—Hillary. Bill said: "Hillary's selection guarantees that I will have a person who is closer to me than anyone else overseeing a project that is more important than anything else. I don't know if it's a politically wise move, but it's the right thing to do."

Among the committee's recommendations were mandatory kindergarten, smaller class sizes, longer school years, more school counselors, competency tests, and more class credits required for high school graduation. The proposed standards were enthusiastically supported by most educators. Bill called for an emergency session of the Arkansas legislature to consider turning the recommendations into laws.

The most controversial aspect of the new education plan was how to pay for it. Bill saw no option but to raise the state sales tax, and to dedicate the money to education. To make the tax burden fairer he also proposed to raise corporate taxes and to tax dues paid to country clubs. Bill wanted to make education reform the financial responsibility of all Arkansans.

The established interests fought back. Gas and oil producers, a large industry in Arkansas, stopped the corporate tax increase. The country club tax was defeated. The only tax increase to survive was the sales tax, which disproportionately hurt poor people. However, the sales tax was easier to pass because Arkansas law requires a two-thirds majority of the legislature to increase income taxes, but only one-third to increase sales taxes.

Bill was faced with a dilemma. If he did not allow the sales tax to go through, his dreams for improved education in Arkansas were over. If he let the sales tax pass, then the people who could least afford to pay would have to carry the tax burden. He did not veto the sales tax. Bill knew from his own life that a good education was the best way for people to lift themselves out of poverty. He thought he was doing the right thing.

Just as the controversy over the sales tax was dying down, Bill was criticized by another group. Teachers had been his biggest supporters. But when he decided teachers should take a competency test, the educators rebelled. Bill felt that the people of Arkansas would more easily pay higher taxes if they were confident the money was being spent for qualified teachers. Although he was certain of the abilities of the vast majority of teachers, he said the test was "a small price to pay for the biggest tax increase in the history of the state and to restore the teaching profession to the position of public esteem that I think it deserves."

The teachers, however, felt differently. Many of them let their unhappiness with the competency test be known. Suddenly Bill was faced with losing his biggest supporters. Teachers threatened to desert him in the next election.

Bill was adamant. When the Arkansas Education Association (AEA) worked to stop the competency test from becoming law, Bill said he would kill the tax increase and deny teachers their raise if the test were not put into place.

Bill won the fight; the teacher testing law was passed. But many people believed he had destroyed his political career. When the AEA threatened to boycott the tests, Bill spoke to their state convention and asked them not to put their interests above education reform. The teachers refused to applaud when he finished his speech.

The controversy over the teacher testing law continued during the 1984 campaign. That year brought an even bigger problem for Bill, one that struck much closer to home. The State Police told Bill that his younger brother, Roger, was dealing drugs. In addition, Roger was an addict.

Roger had not negotiated life as easily as his older brother. Bill had made peace with their father before he died, and had only experimented with marijuana a couple of times as a college student. Roger, however, had dropped out of college and began taking drugs while trying to start a career as a rhythm and blues guitarist.

Bill's heart broke for his brother, and for the grief he knew Roger's arrest would cause their mother. It would have been understandable if Bill had sought some way to deal with his brother's problem privately, such as warning Roger, or by sending him to a rehabilitation clinic. An arrest would certainly be used by Bill's enemies. But Bill knew he had to do the right thing. He refused to intervene. Roger was convicted for trafficking in narcotics, and served a year in prison.

Roger was initially bitter at Bill for not shielding him from arrest. Later, however, he realized Bill may have saved his life. "He knew it was going to be better for me," Roger has said. "Had [Bill] not made that decision [to allow the arrest to go through], I was a short leap away from death." Roger thinks he would have continued dealing and abusing drugs.

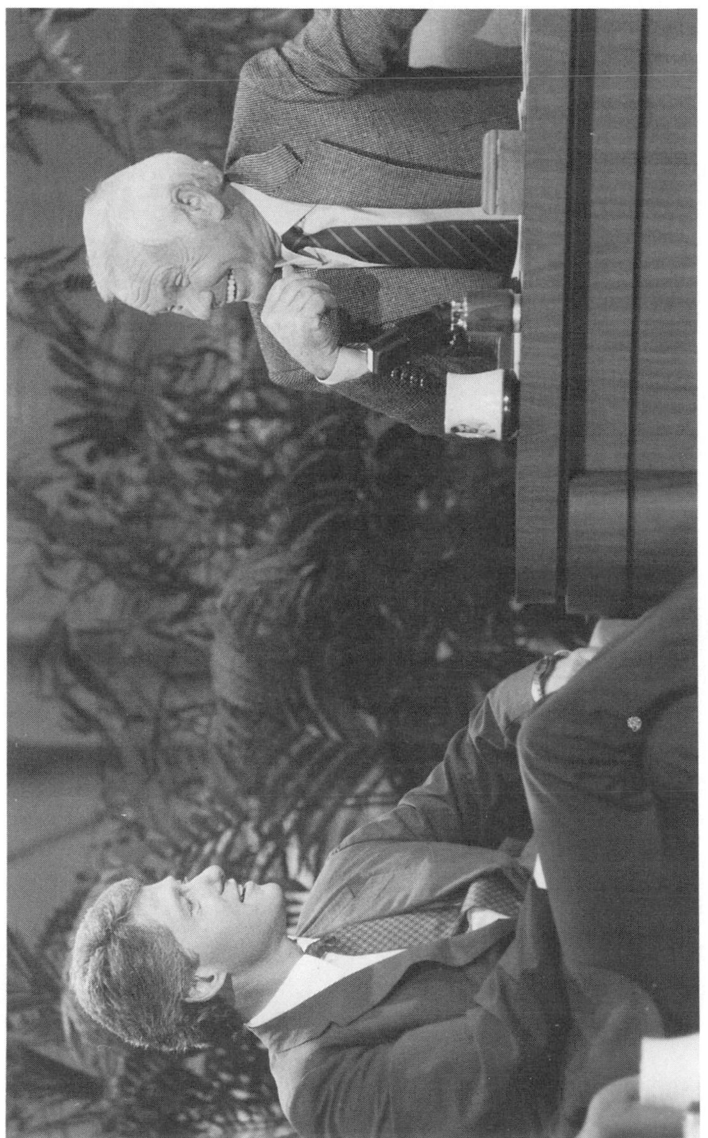

Bill's appearance on "The Tonight Show starring Johnny Carson" helped him regain confidence and popularity after his disastrous nomination speech for Michael Dukakis in 1988.

The story has a happy ending. After his time in prison, Roger was able to kick his habit. He moved to California and got a job as an production assistant on the popular television series "Designing Women." He also formed a rock and roll band.

Even with his brother's arrest, and the opposition of organized teacher's groups, Bill won reelection in 1984.

Although they had failed to defeat Bill, the AEA still insisted their membership would boycott the competency test. Bill warned teachers they would be replaced if they refused to take the test. On testing day, March 23, 1985, the boycott failed. The vast majority of teachers showed up at test sites. All but 3.5% of the teachers passed the test.

Bill had won his fight and shown that he would oppose even his supporters if a program were in the best interest of his state. Later, the AEA made peace with Bill. Today, teachers are again among Bill's strongest supporters.

Bill's work for education brought him national attention. He appeared on such television shows as "Face The Nation," "This Week With David Brinkley," and "Donahue." Along with Bruce Babbitt of Arizona, Mario Cuomo of New York, Lamar Alexander of Tennessee, and Michael Dukakis of Massachusetts, Bill was viewed as a potential national leader.

In 1985, Bill told a reporter "it would be fun to run [for president], even if you lost. It would be a challenge to go out and meet the people and try to communicate your ideas and bring the different parts of the country together."

Bill became more active in the National Governors Association, and was elected chairman in 1986. But, even as his national reputation grew, Bill kept his attention on his job at home. He continued to work for economic growth. He traveled to Japan and other countries to encourage investment in Arkansas.

Bill was concerned with the future of the Democratic Party. Along with other leaders, he was upset by Walter Mondale's devastating defeat by Ronald Reagan in the 1984 presidential race. It seemed the image of the Democratic Party had to be changed if it were to win national elections. With this in mind, Bill joined a group of moderate Democrats called The Democratic Leadership Council (DLC) to help the party focus on the real needs of people. His active participation in the DLC brought Bill even more national exposure, and allowed him to meet Democrats from other parts of the country.

Even with his busy schedule, Bill maintained his relationship with Chelsea. He drove her to school every morning he was in Little Rock. "The morning is our time," he told friends. Chelsea was an excellent student, able to skip a grade in school. She loved ballet and danced in recitals from an early age. Bill was always present for her ballet recitals, cheered for her softball team, and took her to the movies. Passers-by were often amused to see Bill, Chelsea and Hillary playing touch football on the mansion lawn.

The Clintons were an unconventional First Family, treating the governor's mansion as a personal home as well as an official residence. One night, Ernest Green and his wife called on the mansion rather late. Ernest had gained national attention as one of the nine black students to integrate Little Rock High School in 1957. He had graduated and gone on to become an attorney, and was a good friend of the Clintons. When the Greens rang the bell, Hillary and Bill greeted them in their bathrobes and immediately invited the couple to join them for a midnight snack in the kitchen.

This informality was typical of the Clintons. In fact, most social activities were centered around the kitchen, where they would invite friends to try out new recipes. At other times, they would sing songs around the piano, or play board and card games. The most frequent dinner companions, however, were Bill's mother and stepfather, and, after they moved to

Little Rock in 1987, Hillary's parents.

The Clintons also developed a warm friendship with Eliza Jane Ashley, the cook at the mansion for over 30 years. Bill and Hillary always invited her to the Christmas open house and frequently took her to church on Christmas Eve and to dinner on Easter. Ms. Ashley often referred to the youthful governor as her "adopted son." Their relationship was so close that she felt no hesitation in suggesting to the Clintons that they have a child. "I said to the governor, 'It's time for you to have some children before you get too old,' " she recalls. Bill answered, "If the Lord sees fit for us to, we will." Shortly after their conversation, the Clintons told Ms. Ashley there soon would be a baby in the mansion. "We were all on cloud nine," Ms. Ashley remembers.

The Clintons were hard workers and frequent travelers during their twelve years in the governor's mansion. "We would serve them at night," the cook recalls. "Sometimes, they wouldn't even be there. We'd just leave the meals."

The Clintons have strong religious convictions, although there was a period when Bill drifted away from the Baptist faith of his youth. Hillary remained true to her Methodist upbringing; thus, the Clintons attended different churches in Little Rock. Hillary explained their unusual behavior as her not wishing to impose her beliefs upon her husband, a trait she also appreciated in Bill. Arkansans accepted it as just another quirk of their unique First Family. Bill and Hillary left the choice up to Chelsea as to which church she would attend. When it came time for confirmation, Chelsea chose the Methodists.

When the Clintons went out socially, it was usually for a combination of politics and Mexican food with friends at Doe's Eat Place in Little Rock, near the capitol.

Friendship is important to both Bill and Hillary. Old friends Diane Blair and actress Mary Steenburgen have seen the Clintons through good times and bad, including listening sympathetically to both during a troubled time in their marriage. Patty Criner, who attended school with Bill, drove Hillary to be with Bill's mother when his second stepfather, Jim Dwire, died.

Acquaintances like Bill's down-home friendliness. "He doesn't have any snobbery or sense that some people are more important than others," reflects one friend. "When he says that we don't have a person to waste in this country, he means it from the bottom of his heart."

Bill also works hard to stay in contact with his

Bill's June 1992 appearance on the popular Arseno Hall show, and his saxophone rendention of "Heartbreak Hotel," helped show a lighter side to the candidate.

Bill and Vice-Presidential running mate Senator Al Gore take an early-morning run.

friends. Always outgoing, Bill has made an immense number of friends over the years. He has the quality of maintaining old friendships even while making new friends. The Tuesday lunches he had with old high school friends were a favorite part of his week in Little Rock.

One friend from high school told reporters during the 1992 campaign of how Bill had surprised her by showing up at her father's funeral in 1987. Her father died in a distant town, and because she knew that Bill was very busy, she decided not to mention her loss to Bill. But when she arrived at the church for the funeral, Bill was there sitting in a pew, ready to comfort her during her time of loss.

Although he is a warm and loving friend, Bill is quite competitive when it comes to games and sports. He loves Trivial Pursuit, Pictionary, and other board games, as well as card games. When he plays with his friends it is with the same intensity he approaches all aspects of his life. But he is always well mannered, never allowing his competitive nature to overcome his friendliness. He has also maintained his lifelong love of all types of music. His taste ranges from classical, to gospel, jazz and, of course, Elvis Presley. The Secret Service code name for him is Elvis.

In 1986, Bill won another election as Governor of Arkansas. This time, his term would run for four years. Although he worked hard on recruiting industry to the state and on education, Bill spent more and more time on the national political stage. He spoke out so often on national issues, and was so involved in the national Democratic Party, many expected him to run for President in 1988.

President Bill Clinton

At first, 1988 seemed to be the ideal year for Bill to run for president. Ronald Reagan was leaving office. That left the presidency without an incumbent running for reelection for the first time since 1968. Many of Bill's friends and supporters encouraged him to run. Most observers thought he would make the effort. *Newsweek* magazine even claimed to have an inside scoop—Bill was definitely going to enter the race.

But, in July of 1987, Bill shocked everyone by announcing that he was not going to run. His reasons for staying out of the race were personal. "Our daughter is seven," he explained. "She is the most important person in the world to us and our most important responsibility. In order to wage a winning campaign, both Hillary and I would have to leave her for long periods of time. That would not be good for her or for us."

Bill was happy when fellow governor Michael Dukakis of Massachusetts asked him to put his name in nomination during the Democratic Convention. Dukakis needed to have a high-profile Southerner speak on his behalf. However, the speech would almost end Bill's own chances for national office.

Because he usually researches and writes his own speeches, Bill rarely needs a prepared script. Minutes before he walked to the podium, Dukakis campaign workers handed him speech, and insisted that he read it exactly as written. Against his better judgement, Bill agreed.

Bill delivered the speech in a hesitant, awkward manner. The large crowd was impatient for Dukakis to appear. The speech took 33 minutes to deliver. Bill had to stop several times and ask for quiet. The only applause he received was when he said the words, "in conclusion." Bill was embarrassed before millions of television viewers, many of whom were getting their first look at him. One television commentator said, "I am afraid Bill Clinton, one of the most attractive governors, just put a blot on his record." Bill later told the press, "It was one of those fluky things. I fell on

The Clintons and Al and Tipper Gore wave to well-wishers at the start of a six-state bus tour shortly after the Democratic Convention.

Bill and Hillary are all smiles after Clinton swept six of eight states in the March 1992 "Super Tuesday" primary elections.

my sword."

Bill was suddenly a national joke. A *Washington Post* story about the speech was entitled "The Numb and the Restless." Johnny Carson called Bill "a windbag" in his opening monologue on the "Tonight Show."

If Bill's first real national exposure was as the butt of jokes, Americans soon had an opportunity to see him in a better light. Johnny Carson invited him to appear on his show, and Bill accepted. Johnny introduced Bill with a long, rambling spiel which started the audience laughing. The young governor entered, laughing right along with the audience. When Johnny pretended to be timing Bill's answers to his questions, he threw his head back and laughed. Johnny asked him if he were planning on a bigger political career in the future and Bill quipped, "That depends on how well I do here tonight." He finished his visit by playing "Summertime" on the saxophone with the Doc Severinson band. When he left the stage, Carson praised him for his sense of humor, and was obviously impressed. Bill later said, "We got lemons, and we made lemonade."

After George Bush won the 1988 presidential campaign, Bill was among the potential Democratic candidates for 1992. In 1989, Bill co-chaired a national summit on education at the request of President Bush, and in 1990 he was elected chairman of the Democratic Leadership Council. *Time* magazine listed him, along with Governor Mario Cuomo of New York and Senator Bill Bradley of New Jersey, as the top Democratic candidates.

In 1990, Bill became the first person to win five terms as governor of Arkansas. It was his toughest race since 1982. His opponent, Sheffield Nelson, accused him of neglecting Arkansas' needs as he pursued national political plans. Bill admitted publicly the "fire" for another term no longer burned in him. In answer to attacks he was only biding his time until he ran for president, Bill pointed out that President Bush was very popular. Political observers thought Bush was probably unbeatable in 1992. When the Iraqi army surrendered to end the Persian Gulf War in the spring of 1991, Bush's popularity rose to nearly 90% in the opinion polls. Most presumed Democratic candidates, such as Al Gore of Tennessee and Bill Bradley, announced they would not run in 1992.

Bill quietly pondered running for president during the spring and summer of 1991. There were considerations other than political factors motivating him. While he supported President Bush in his determination to make Iraqi troops leave Kuwait, Bill was worried by Bush's apparent neglect of urgent domestic problems. As more people lost their jobs, the country was slipping further into economic recession. Health care costs were rising dramatically. These and other problems were piling up while Bush devoted his attention to foreign policy.

Bill sensed many Americans shared his concern over the direction the country was taking. Although President Bush was popular because of his handling of the Persian Gulf conflict, Bill believed people would respond to a candidate who focused attention on domestic problems.

Finally, after a restless night in late summer of 1991, Bill woke up, turned to Hillary, and asked if he should run for president. A sleepy Hillary replied, "You've got to do it." Bill agreed. He was going to be a candidate for President of the United States.

On October 3, 1991, Bill Clinton stood before the historic Old State House in Little Rock and told an audience of 5,000 supporters that he was entering the Presidential race. "I refuse to sit by and let our children become part of the first generation to do worse than their parents," he said. "I don't want my child or your child to be part of a country that's coming apart instead of coming together."

He continued to say that America was "headed in the wrong direction, slipping behind, losing our way," because of twelve years of Republican leadership. He promised to provide a plan for affordable health care, and a plan to help people attend college or vocational school. "We need a new covenant to rebuild America," he said. "It's just common sense. Government's responsibility is to provide more opportunity. The people's responsibility is to make the most of it."

Bill was off and running.

The other major candidates in the race were former California Governor Jerry Brown, Senator Bob Kerrey of Nebraska, former Massachusetts Senator Paul Tsongas, Iowa Senator Tom Harkin, and Virginia Governor Douglas Wilder.

The New Hampshire primary was the first big race of the election year. That state turned out to be a perfect place for Bill to make a case for his candidacy. New Hampshire is a small state, which allowed Bill to make personal contact with many voters. Democrats were impressed with his deep knowledge of issues, and his ability to answer their questions thoroughly without resorting to notes. Word quickly spread throughout New Hampshire, and eventually the rest of the country, that Bill was the most exciting of the Democratic candidates. Bill rose high in the New Hampshire polls.

New Hampshire is where Bill got the reputation of being a "policy wonk," someone obsessed with having a clearly-defined position on every subject. The term was given to him by reporters. Bill earned the label by giving long, highly detailed answers to questions. Also, his answers made it clear he had spent years studying the issues. Reporters who followed the campaign thought Bill's long answers would bore voters. However, as the campaign developed, many observers were surprised to discover that the voters were indeed paying close attention. Two months before the primary, Bill led in the polls.

Then the world seemed to cave in on top of Bill—and on Hillary and Chelsea. A supermarket tabloid ran a story alleging that Bill had a long-term affair with a woman in Arkansas named Gennifer Flowers. Ms. Flowers had always denied earlier rumors about she and Bill. But in the tabloid article, she said she had been Bill's mistress for over ten years. When the national news media picked up the story, many people thought Bill's short run for the presidency was over.

Bill refused to give up. He and Hillary appeared on the CBS program "60 Minutes" and flatly denied the affair with Ms. Flowers. He also made it clear that his marriage was a private matter, and he was not going to answer any more questions about his personal life.

When the interviewer, Steve Kroft, seemed to imply that Bill and Hillary had worked out "an arrangement" in their marriage, Bill shot back: "You're looking at two people who love each other. This is not an arrangement or an understanding. This is a marriage."

Hillary was uncharacteristically open about her private life as she described for the press the mutual respect and common ideals that had solidified their marriage over the years. "It's that sense of believing in something and committing yourself to something," says Hillary. "That was the great basis of our relationship when we first met. We recognized it in each other. It's a compelling sense of what we have, about what we're meant to do and what life is meant to be."

The response to Bill's appearance was mostly positive. Although the allegations of infidelity had hurt him in New Hampshire, Bill went right back to the campaign. His poll numbers began climbing again. It looked as if he had survived a blow that would have driven others out of the race.

Then, on February 6, less than two weeks before the New Hampshire primary, *The Wall Street Journal* suggesting that Bill had dodged the draft during the Vietnam War. A few days later Ted Koppel, of the ABC news program "Nightline," called the Clinton campaign and told them he had a copy of a letter Bill had written to the director of the University of Arkansas ROTC program back in 1969. In the letter, Bill thanked the ROTC director for "saving me from the draft."

Bill and his advisors held a series of long meetings. Some suggested that he drop out. The candidate had to decide if the pressure and the bad publicity would damage Hillary and Chelsea. Chelsea had held up well during the Gennifer Flowers controversy, even telling her parents that she was proud of them for their courage. But a concerted attack on her father's patriotism would not be easy to withstand. Bill had another tough decision to make. He finally decided it would be intolerable if the American people labeled him a quitter. He decided to stay in the race.

Bill appeared on "Nightline" while Ted Koppel read the letter. Afterward, Bill answered Koppel's questions by explaining he had joined ROTC to avoid going to Vietnam, felt badly about his decision, and then put his name back in the draft. When his lottery number was drawn, it was high enough to keep him from being drafted, and enabled him to continue his education.

The draft issue was more harmful to Bill's candidacy than the Gennifer Flowers controversy. The

Vietnam War had been a painful and bitter experience for the entire country. Many people thought failure to serve during a war, even on grounds of conscience, was unforgivable. Others, however, believed the war was wrong and did not resent Bill's failure to serve. Bill reacted to this crisis as he had to earlier ones. He went back to New Hampshire and campaigned almost around the clock. Aides literally collapsed from exhaustion, while Bill looked for another hand to shake, another question to answer.

Hard work and determination paid off. Bill came in second in the critical primary. Only New Hampshire neighbor Paul Tsongas did better. On primary night Bill surprised the news media by going on TV to claim victory. "New Hampshire, tonight, has made Bill Clinton the Comeback Kid," he claimed. "I just can't wait now to take this campaign across the country. I cannot wait to win the nomination."

Most "experts" had expected Bill to concede defeat after his second place finish. But his appearance on national television allowed the public to see an enthusiastic fighter who was not ready to be counted out. Appearing on television earlier than the actual winner, Paul Tsongas, and declaring victory, turned out to be a master stroke of strategy.

The early "victory" speech was Hillary's idea. As pressure mounted on Bill, Hillary began exerting

A typical campaign photo of Bill, in the midst of a crowd shaking hands, at a rally in Maryland during the presidential campaign.

During debate with George Bush and Ross Perot.

more and more influence over the campaign. This new role brought her into the public spotlight. Hillary was a new type of political wife. The smart, successful lawyer who made no excuses for being her husband's top advisor became a campaign issue. Bill's enemies tried to make her a point of controversy, claiming she represented a new type of woman who put her career before the traditional roles of mother and wife.

Hillary was unruffled by the criticism and maintained a hectic schedule. After the New Hampshire primary, she usually campaigned in a different state than Bill, working hard to build up support. Even with all the travel, the couple sought to maintain a family life. Both Bill and Hillary tried to be home in Arkansas every other weekend to spend time with Chelsea. "This is the hardest part of the campaign,"Hillary said. "We have never spent this kind of time away from her."

Bill alleviated some of the sadness he felt at being away from Chelsea by calling her every night, often assisting her with Algebra homework. Sometimes he even faxed her help on difficult problems.

A low point of the campaign for Hillary occurred when she commented that she was not ashamed of pursuing her career. "I guess I could have stayed at home and baked cookies and held teas," she said. Immediately, Bill's opponents claimed Hillary was ridiculing women who did not work outside the home. The Republicans, who were launching a "family values" campaign theme, accused her of being "anti-family." Hillary, realizing she may have offended women who chose to become housewives and homemakers, made a public apology. "There is nothing," she said, "in my life or work that could be constructed as disparaging women who choose to stay home and raise a family. I honor them. Those are the choices my own mother made." Her popularity in the polls began to rise.

Despite the barrage of attacks, Bill and Hillary kept campaigning. At every stop, and in every speech, Bill talked about helping the middle class, of reforming education and health care, and investing in the economy of the United States. He won primary after primary.

Although Bill was on his way to wrapping up the Democratic nomination for President, he was still trailing badly in the opinion polls. In the spring, Texas billionaire Ross Perot began his unusual presidential campaign and received extensive media coverage. Perhaps the lowest point in the entire campaign was, ironically, the night Bill wrapped up the nomination by winning the California primary. Newspapers the next morning headlined that Ross Perot was leading in the national polls. Bill was a distant third. No one seemed to notice his victory in California. Many political analysts claimed the race was only between Ross Perot and George Bush. Some Democrats, convinced he could not win, publicly discussed the idea of asking Bill to step aside. It seemed the Gennifer Flowers and draft evasion stories had crippled Bill's chances for victory.

It was time for unconventional methods. Late night talk show host Arsenio Hall had impressed Bill as a crusader against drug abuse, an issue close to Bill's heart. When Hall asked Bill to appear on the show, he agreed.

Hall opened his show that night with a new member of the band. Bill, wearing a blue suit and dark glasses, played a rip-roaring version of "Heartbreak Hotel" with the band. The audience went wild. After the song, Bill talked with Hall and impressed everyone with his candor and charm.

Bill made another successful move in choosing Tennessee Senator Al Gore as his vice-presidential running mate. A fellow southern moderate, Gore was an unusual choice. Most presidential candidates pick running mates from a different section of the country,

New President-elect Bill Clinton speaks to a happy crowd on the night of his election win over George Bush.

so that the ticket has geographical balance and can attract voters from more than one region. But Gore was a highly-respected legislator, a leader on environmental issues, and another member of the post-World War II generation. The selection proved to be a popular one.

Bill steadily moved up in the polls. His next big boost came during the July Democratic National Convention, held in Madison Square Garden in New York City. The convention started successfully, but a dark cloud hung over the first three days. Ross Perot was still high in the polls, and threatened to disrupt any chance Bill had of unseating an incumbent president. Then, on the last day of the convention, a few hours before Bill was scheduled to deliver his acceptance speech, Perot held a news conference in his hometown of Dallas, Texas and announced he was leaving the race. He cited the reinvigorated Democratic Party, under Bill's leadership, as the reason he was dropping out.

Later that night, Bill gave a strong speech accepting his party's nomination. The next day he and Hillary, along with Al Gore and his wife Tipper, left New York for a highly publicized thousand-mile bus trip across the Midwest.

On the bus trip, Bill and Al Gore became an effective political team. During long rides between stops, and in morning jogging sessions, they discovered many shared values. When making campaign speeches, Gore never failed to make it clear he was "in synch" with the presidential candidate, and Bill repeatedly told the press their close association would continue in the Clinton Administration. One reporter characterized their friendship by playing upon a recent popular movie; he called their campaign “Bill and Al's Excellent Adventure.”

Never before had a presidential and vice-presidential candidate campaigned so closely together. Bill and Al traveled and relaxed together, telling good-natured jokes at campaign stops. Bill said he intended to give the office of vice-president a power and influence it had never had.

Just as Bill and Al became good friends, a friendship developed between their wives early in the campaign. One campaign worker remembers that “Tipper Gore and Hillary immediately hit it off on a personal level, talking about themselves and their families.” Tipper described the friendship as one between two “long-lost sisters.” The campaign was once described as an “extended double date.” Tipper's genuine friendship helped to dispel the argument that Hillary was a ruthless career woman uninterested in her family. Tipper chose to stay with her children rather than seek a career outside the home, and she helped found a group that was successful in convincing the music industry to add warning labels on products with sexually explicit or violent rock lyrics. She shared many values with Hillary, and had no problems with Hillary's views.

After the convention and the bus trip, Bill's popularity soared in the polls, until he was leading President Bush by as many as thirty points. Although Perot reentered the race a month before the election, he never restored himself as a leading candidate.

Bill worked hard to maintain his lead. Having experienced blows during the New Hampshire primary which would have knocked other people out of the race, Bill sensed that in 1992 the voters were concerned mostly about the economy and their children's futures. They did not want to be distracted by personal attacks on the candidates. He focused his campaign on explaining his ideas for improving people's lives.

President Bush, however, was shocked at how quickly he fell in public opinion. Never had a president fallen so quickly and so far in the polls. However, the reason for Bush's decline was simple. Things seemed to be getting worse economically, as unemployment rose and the budget deficit widened. And

President Bush seemed slow to realize people were worried about their future; when he did, the solutions he offered were not popular.

For help with the presidential campaign, Bill and Hillary once again called upon Tony and Hugh Rodham, who traveled to Florida, Pennsylvania, and Illinois stumping for Bill. Their infectious, gregarious personalities made them popular with the media and the crowds, although they found it hard not to respond aggressively to the increasing attacks on Hillary in the news media. She advised them to ignore the attacks, saying "It's just politics."

But the attacks hurt. Republicans portrayed Hillary as a "radical," or aggressive, feminist. Political opponents tried to show her as a model of how the "modern woman" was destroying "family values," partly because she "preferred the boardroom to the kitchen."

Hillary realized the attacks were designed to cause concern among voters who might otherwise vote for Bill, but were opposed to the idea of "an activist" First Lady. Past articles she had written on children's rights were distorted in the "anti-Hillary" campaign. In them, she supposedly had compared marriage to slavery, and encouraged children to sue their parents. Charges were also made that she would assert influence over her husband on the issues of homosexual rights, abortion, and women in combat.

Hillary was sometimes unfavorably compared to Barbara Bush, whose grandmotherly image was highly popular. Hillary responded to the criticism by saying, "I really don't know what to make of it. What has happened has been part of a very sad and cynical political strategy. It's not really about me."

Hillary continued, "There's that kind of double bind women find themselves in. On the one hand, be smart, and stand up for yourself. On the other hand, don't offend anyone and don't step on toes, or you'll become somebody who no one likes because you are too assertive."

Despite all the political campaigns she had gone through with Bill, and her years as a governor's wife, Hillary was unprepared for the rigors of the presidential campaign. She felt a need to return to Little Rock to "make a cup of tea, hang out with Chelsea, take an afternoon nap. If I don't get back home, I don't feel grounded," she said.

Hillary worked to protect her family during the grueling campaign. She refused to let Chelsea be interviewed, and was guarded about photographs of her daughter. To assure Bill time to think and rest, Hillary reorganized the campaign schedule. She reviewed Bill's speeches, and helped decide what issues should be emphasized. When the press began poking fun at Bill's fondness for fast food, and his expanding waistline, Hillary put him on a diet and personally prepared his food to help him trim his weight.

Bill offered to debate both President Bush and Ross Perot. After a series of negotiations, a ten day period in mid-October was selected for three debates. Bill was eager to present his case for changing the direction of the country.

The first debate, held at Washington University in St. Louis, Missouri, was in the traditional style. The candidates stood behind podiums and answered questions from a panel of reporters. Bill appeared a little nervous, but was able to give convincing answers to the questions. When the event was over, polls indicated most people believed either Bill or Ross Perot had won.

The second debate, held four days later in Richmond, Virginia, turned out to be the most memorable, partly because of the unusual format. During the primary campaign, Bill was at his best answering direct questions from assembled voters. He insisted the second debate follow this format, allowing the audience to ask the questions. Often Bill approached the audience members asking questions and looked them directly in the eye while delivering his answer.

President Bush came to the debate prepared to criticize Bill for protesting the Vietnam War 25 years before. When the audience expressed disinterest in hearing the candidates attack each other, Bush seemed confused. During the debate, he looked at his watch several times, as though anxious for the debate to end. When a young woman asked Bush how the recession had personally affected him, he seemed unable to give a clear answer. Most political analysts agreed Bill easily won the second debate.

President Bush did better in the final debate, held in East Lansing, Michigan, where a return to the more traditional format allowed him to belittle Bill as "a failed Governor of a small state." But, it was too late. The second debate probably secured the election for Bill. Voters were impressed by his answers and his confident style.

On November 3, 1992, William Jefferson Clinton was elected the 42nd President of the United States. He won most of the major states to gain an overwhelming majority in the Electoral College, while winning 43% of the popular vote in a three-way race. His lifetime of energetic commitment had been rewarded with the nation's highest political office. He was the second youngest man ever elected President.

Bill won the presidency for many reasons. It is

clear that he truly cares for people's welfare. He is a man who has maintained friendships since childhood, and this has kept him close to his roots. Bill has a strong commitment to his family, his religious faith, and a belief in the greatness of the United States of America. He is convinced America can go on to even greater accomplishments. His hard work and determination have deeply impressed the citizens of his country.

During the campaign, Bill dedicated himself to solve several serious problems facing the country. One important issue is the rapid increase in health care costs. Bill has promised to present a program which would provide medical care at reasonable costs to all Americans. Also, in a rapidly changing economic world, Bill believes students must learn skills which prepare them for the future. The key to education reform lies in retraining people for new careers if their old jobs are made obsolete by technological changes.

The most critical problem facing the country today is the huge national debt (money borrowed by the United States to run the government) accumulated over the last 25 years. Bill realizes if the debt is not controlled, little can be done about other national problems.

The role Hillary plays in the Clinton Administration promises to create a new role for the First Lady. However, she will not be the first presidential wife to play an active role in government. Rosalyn Carter attended cabinet meetings. Bess Truman helped write some of Harry's best speeches. Edith Wilson played a crucial role in her husband Woodrow's second term, by handling correspondence during his long illness. Eleanor Roosevelt spoke out on many social issues. Betty Ford lobbied for the Equal Rights Amendment.

Hillary will have a more public role. This became evident during the economic conference Bill held in Little Rock weeks before taking office. Her role during the televised conference reminded insiders of her performance as chair of the governor's task force on education. Later, she was one of only five advisors in the room when Bill considered candidates for cabinet positions. Members of the "transition team" were impressed with her knowledge of government, saying "she knows more about this stuff than most of us do." Bill has promised Hillary will chair a commission to study the nation's health care crisis.

1992 was known as the "Year of the Woman" because of the historically large number of women elected to Congress, and the prominence of "women's issues" in many campaigns. Hillary promises to be an advocate on issues about which many of the newly elected female representatives are also concerned.

Chelsea will perhaps face the greatest adjustment of any Clinton family member. No one can shield her from criticism directed to her father. She will also have to live the constrained lifestyle forced upon children in the White House.

Although public school advocates hoped the Clintons would enroll Chelsea in a District of Columbia public school, Bill and Hillary chose Sidwell Friends School for their daughter's education. There it will be easier for the Secret Service to protect her.

Bill and Hillary are determined to bring a new style to the White House. Rather than just be the President and First Lady, they intend to be the "First Couple," and together make a significant contribution toward solving the country's problems.

This desire to change tradition also extends to the personal level. Many presidents have allowed the office to distance them from their friends. Bill is determined not to allow this to happen. He is a dedicated jogger who, as a governor, often stopped running to talk to people on the street. The Secret Service hopes he will be content to use the recreational facilities of the White House and Camp David, the presidential retreat in Maryland. But Washington residents may see the President of the United States jogging through the streets of the capitol.

Clearly, Bill Clinton promises to be a different type of president, who will bring a new spirit to the office. He combines a winning personality with the political skills necessary to successfully govern. Hopefully, his efforts to improve government will improve the lives of average Americans.

No one knows what the future will bring for America. But William Jefferson Clinton of Arkansas has proven, publicly and privately, that he has the personal qualities needed to deal with whatever fate may hold in store.